POETRY NOW

NORTHERN IRELAND

1992

First published in Great Britain in 1992 by
POETRY NOW
4 Hythegate, Werrington,
Peterborough, PE4 7ZP

All the poems in this book are printed on 100% recycled paper.

Contents

Return Journey

Grey smudge on the horizon
Why so powerful?
Land of my fathers calling me home.
Great brooding mountains,
clear, dancing streams;
the essence of your majesty sings in my heart.

Wind tearing through my hair
stealing my breath and my thoughts.
Sea exploding
beneath huge crashing weight of metal.
Gulls jeering in effortless flight.
'Turn again,' they say, 'turn back.'

Grey smudge on the horizon
quietly appealing.
Land of my children calling me home.
Small rolling drumlins
Flat wastes of water
Warmth of your welcome:
Yes,
I will return.

Jean Withers

My People - Ireland

Quaint and characterful
Like a timber barn where livestock lay
In damp, dank hay,
Created last summer.
Rugged, craggy facial lines
Bronzed in weather-beaten tone.
Each crevasse, a hidden tale,
Secretive and dark
Never to be known.

Hands of work and toil,
Not smooth, or calm
Like her rivers'
Silent ripples flow,
Sweat lines, on the palm.
Their stance unmoveable.
Feet, to walk one way,
To help, to defend,
To love, to remember
The blooded battlefield
Where loved ones lay.

Summer sun sets
On the longest night
Disappearing to another time.
Her memory fades
But never leaves
Her ever ageing mind.
Quaint and characterful
Like a timber barn where livestock lay
In damp, dank hay,
Created last summer.

G Keith Henderson

Robin

I stared at him; he
Cocked his dainty head
And stared right back; and
All the wide green leafy world
Around me shrank and
Was encapsulated by
One tiny
Toy like black and
Shiny
Button of an eye.

Clement Murray

Afraid

Lying legs wide apart exposed to
cold unwanted outside sharpness.

A lonely child below a stone statue
pain shoots through a body so young
torn apart from giving birth.

Crying out for help from the Virgin
mother what holy thing would let them
die?

She hides bearing the child on cold
wet unyielding earth.

Shame makes her scurry away fear of
priests cross-faced, frustrated, collared,
Old men.

Who know nothing of love of sex of
feeling unwanted unforgiving of a moment
of weakness.

Is this child so bad that she would
rather die in a field than ask for
help.

Praying to the Virgin Queen cold and still
she lay cold and still, dead a baby in her arms,
blue and unwanted.

Suffer little children for you know not
what you do,
and they don't want you to know.

Frankie Quinn

Aspiration

I still aspire that I may yet create
Poetic fire; and pen a phrase
To stimulate a part
Of some receptive heart.

To boldly bare my secret soul
That someone there may care
The hidden thoughts I dare
To show for other eyes to know:
And having read perhaps may care
To muse on all I say and would convey
Rejoiced to find a kindred mind.

And on some distant day recall a line,
A word of mine, to cause
A busy hand to pause...
An eye to see with memory...
And in that reverie
Remember me.

Ralph McMurray

An Afternoon in Spring

They roll and toll,
Spilling over each other
Creating scenarios
Unexplainable.
Steep steps in the sky, layer a blanket,
Protecting.
Old masters of life.
Deciding the seas.
Patterns of time.
Changing how we feel, colouring our lives
Grey to red.
A mixture of turning turmoil.
Turbulence.
Bursting - wet soft rain,
Enclosing us
Protecting.
Always supporting the air,
The unseen in us.

Roisin Carville

The Gargoyles of Coal

The gargoyles of coal spit flames and lines of smoke through the bars.
The rest of the fire grumbles on, unaware of the protestations at the front.
They speak and shriek and scrape me with their tongues of scorn,
The rest of the fire grumbles on.
The light burns my limbs and makes them sore,
I have to move away to protect myself.
They will shout louder and display their strength,
And brand their crucifix on my hand, should I ... try to extinguish them.
A lick of one tongue upon my neck, another on my cheek.
Like a lovers symbol of final initiation - a member

Lucia Thornton

Thoughts of Legahory Bomb Victim

Last Thursday night we went to Mass,
as I felt the need to pray,
for the safety of my family,
through these worrying winter days.

The music was soft and gentle
Like the words of the carol we sang,
the words were 'Lord hear our prayer'
before that terrible bang.

In the deathly silence that followed,
before the roof came crashing down,
our hearts were frozen with horror
I thought the end of our days had come.

A miracle took place before the eyes
of every person there,
No one killed or seriously injured,
The Lord truly answered our prayer.

Kathleen Shanks

Internecine

I sweated fear
Despite the heady fumes of gin
Anaesthetised
The throb and pulse of Karaoke
Belied what was to come
A man had called me to him
Hissed inanities, he couldn't speak
A drunk sat down beside him

I found him in the foyer
Blood and gore besmattered, a broken nose.
Who did it? An age - old feud.
'Tout' he taunted 'R.U.C.!'
and looked as if he'd fight again.
'Fight me my friend aggrieved.

I trailed behind the sadness of all hatred.
I couldn't fathom. 'Mind your business,
We'll sort this from the top!'
He craved my aid and luckily for me
he couldn't quite enunciate.
I stayed away a week.

Such ugliness; God bless you Mother Ireland
In your name gut savagery
Decries the gentleness of song and mists of reverie
'Get back! Get back!' I grieve
Dehumanised.
Outside I vomited

Joe Ryder

Forsythia

A confession of small stars that are more
Glorious than the sun that refuses to shine,
For defying all, they brave the hail that stings my face,
And radiate more golden yellow, than even the
Cloud that lowers and threatens in the far off
Distance, can intimidate into sobriety.
Not even when the eerie howl of Winter wolf
Entwines its way around each delicate branch,
And whispers cold - in icy breath,
The threat of snow and gale,
Can make one fragile bloom return to the bud
Which gave it birth,
And hide away, - dark,
Each beautiful face.

Gwendolyn Wright

Broken Land

Turned on the radio the other day;
Fergie's got the flu
And they're still blowing the shit out of each other
In bloody Belfast -
Who gives a damn anyway?
Not the patriotic Yank
Propping up a Bronx bar,
Drinking emerald beer to tunes of glory -
Pass the bucket Bud
And we'll drop another dollar in the freedom-fighters' piggy bank.

Not the squaddies mum
Who only thinks of little Tommy,
Over there.
In between ironing socks
In sunny Bridlington.
Not the government minister
Who feels obliged to make a speech in the House,
To men fat on suffering.
About that eternal, infernal boil
Called Ulster.

Not the foreign media-man
With his pre-set type-set view
In black and white.
Looking under the cracked pieces
Of an already broken land.
Turned on the radio the other day;
Fergie's got over the flu
And they're still blowing the shit out of each other
In bloody Belfast -
Who gives a damn anyway?

A J Patterson

All That Fear Stuff

The people passing by hurried to their homes,
Hugging their destinies to warm their thin bones.
Then came the patrol of the night,
I took no notice and looked to the sky
'Til I spotted one running to confront,
And the questions just rattles away,
'Where the fuck you going mate?'
I could only hesitate.

I did not imagine any small guilt,
Or the barracks, but they hung in the air,
On the steam of my breath, all that fear stuff,
And behind where I stood with my strange friend
Was the small cenotaph to all those killed,
Terror, threats and dread its living branches.
So we could never escape the battle,
In the streets and back alleys, its trenches,
Now filled with the red wine this was distilled.

The grey marble towered now
Where it had loitered before,
Shake well and you'll wake O'Leary,
Or the thirteen men that were shot,
Who miss the march of this retreating world,
The slow march to the cemetery,
As dusk falls again, here, in Derry.

Stephen Brown

The Awakening

Still heavy with those 'snippets of death'
Returning the cares that left in the night
the weighing of the balances
To see, and investigate if the illumining brings a heavier or much lighter day.
The calling to muster the forces of strength
That throws back the warmth of the snare
To enlist the aid of the cold
It's grip, casts away the mystical haze of the dawning and clarifies the day.
Each piece of clothing conscripted to wear
Symbolically tells of the burden placed on
Before even escaping the den,
There comes the dreaded indictment, 'Today is another new day'
When the morning has not concluded
It's course only neariy run
The trinity of man is commanded, 'Come now return what have you, we, I to
do with this long day.'
Yet some gain the victory over the snare
And carry the inevitable weight
Hours become years encumbering
unassuming the darkness eventually dispels the trauma for another day

Tatty Gordon

Wisdom and Youth

Why does wisdom linger
Till the years have brought us age
Can we not know the way to act
When youth is on the stage
Or must not youth be wise?

Why must experience teach
Could wisdom not bestow
Her gift on youth as well as age
So that youth might know
Can only age be wise

Oh why the wasted years
And all the agonies untold
That might have been avoided
Had but wisdom taken hold
On youth instead of age

Mistakes of others help us not
And sometimes not our own
Can make us do the things we ought
For wisdom is unknown
Till life's best years are gone

When wisdom comes it is to late
To know the way to live
For death, not life for us doth wait
And death will not forgive
The folly of our youth

S John Henderson

A Date for the Older Newly Single Woman

An outwardly placid persona belies internal turmoil
Overshadowing the possibility of enjoyment
Sexy lingerie and Chanel Number Five
Incipient female trappings designed for man
Seem part of the required preparation for this occasion
Where in the past had the roots been imbedded so deep
The fragility of independence wanted yet difficult to deliver
Tottering on the tightrope of affection - a dog
Clinging to the one who deigns to give love
Worshipping the God figure yet espousing
For disciples to believe
In tones not strident but rising with conviction
The gospel of feminism

Mary McPeak

Picnic Site - Portstewart

Satisfied tourists pack up flasks and baskets.
Speculating, loitering noisily overhead
The gull selects his moment
then he swoops and lands below the table,
Snaps up discarded bread
And dunks it in the blood - red puddle in the lay-by.
Strangely, he brings the sop to the table
To share with squawking friends,
His duty done, he takes off, soaring to the west,
Then flies down through the crimson rays,
Becoming a raven crucifix before the fiery sun.
He wheels, flies upwards into light,
Redeemed from fire, his wings turned grey to white.
Purified and mystical like a dove
Again he comes to land.
I knew he would return,
And as he broke some bread, I recognised his features.
Just then, he rose with ease in the air
Up to the sky
A shining transfigurement with outspread wings,
Soaring upwards, on up and out of sight.
I know he will return again.

Mavis Abernethy

The Drowning

Seeking luck through the evening,
He spat into the torn mouth
Of the first fish pulled on board:
Fishes' eyes have seen strange things,
He murmured - the uneasy burden
Of a prophetic word.

With darkness came a listening wind;
The sea made mouths at us all night.
Not until the break of light
Did he come in,
Off Heddles Port -
Pockets inside out,
Mouth full of the ocean's spit.

Suppose what they say is true -
We sink beneath the sea
Lost in the flood of memory:
Then say his last journey
Was no macabre pirouette
Through the watery dark;
But that he,went down serenely,
Rapt, as in a childhood zone,
In the whirling silence of a snowstorm
Under an oval dome.

Adrian Rice

Soldier

I crawl along the pavement, taste its grit,
An abused foetus, sprawled, outstretched.
My finger falls into the cracks,
A wicked pixie tears my slacks,
And burns into my back before my eyes could close,
Now I see my bloodied nose,
A little trickle from my mouth.
I'm watching from a room above,
On the floor a girl is seen, rubbing at her groin,
She is tossed a coin.
It strikes her tear blurred cheek and seems to race
The fingers that now and then hook her face
And try to rip away her pain,
Through us a soldiers tool spits fire and death.

Richard McLernon

The Badger

The first time I saw a badger
it was lying dead on the motorway
a few miles west of Belfast's sprawl
and the notorious Falls.

It could have been an old pullover
glistening with dew but for it's zebra-snout,
its still short legs, the seepage of blood,
black against the grey tar

A cloud-shift and an explosion of light
ignited its eyes, at once brilliant and numinous,
and for a moment I thought it alive,
resurrected and sacrosanct.

Trundling on with the morning's traffic
into the throb of Belfast
I notices a dented bumper, splattered red
car paint or blood? I wonder

Damian Quinn

One Common Bond

He slipped in through the back door,
Nobody seen him arriving.
The fine Christian gent.

'Is he in there?' asked one.
'No I don't think so,
I don't think he's arrived yet.'
Commented another.

'Jasus! he is,
I saw him close the blinds,
how did he get in there without us seeing him.'
Said their mate.
There were weak smiles and tempers frayed,
that morning,
the longest three and a half hours ever.

They all huddled together,
friends and foe.
Everyone had one common bond,
Northern Irish Catholic and Protestant alike.
They were threatened and they knew it.

Hiding behind each other.
Frightened cattle herded into the slaughter house.
Some of them were going.
But, didn't know who first.

Fell, the first victim.
The small, spectacled, charcoal suit,
used the blood red coat like an avenging angel,
on the , 'Dead wood.'
That sat stacked up before him.

One by one they entered an unholy ark.
Knees trembling.
For many, their lives ended.
Each received the dreaded, 'Brown envelope.'
Redundancy money in order.

Out they went as they entered,
one by one.
tool box in hand and on to the scrap heap.
He slipped out through the back door.
Nobody seen him leaving.

'Has he gone? I can't bare to look.'
Said one, meaning the charcoal suit.
'Aye!'
Commented the other sadly,
watching his mate wave good-bye to him,
as he walked out through the front gate.

Paul Gupta

Ireland

There's magic in those Irish hills,
With dancing moving skies.
There is drama in the voices
Of folk as they pass by.
There's whispers in the gentle winds,
And soft dew on your hair.
There is magic in the island,
And mystery in the air.

Marion Chornobrywy

Mr Cooper's Death

I turned left into Union Street
Feeling slightly peeved when I saw
The traffic jammed and army uniforms.
My mind was weighing up the pros and cons
Of buying blouses - this or that.

At the entry to the bus station
Soldiers, police and sniffer dogs
Were moving slowly in an aimless way
U.D.A, R.U.C, U.D.A, R.U.C., U.U.U.U.U.

The cars moved quickly
And I bought my blouse
Pink with white spots,
Oh what joy to take it home and try it on.
While in the yard off Union Street
Limbs, guts, family and blood were smashed and scattered.

'Did you hear there was a bomb in Cookstown?
It's just been on the news.'
'Really!
I thought there must be something going on,
I just went past. What was it?'
'A man called Cooper.'
'Oh.'
'The brother calls for no retaliation.'
Says the television announcer.

'His daughter is in my class.
Samantha-a nice girl. She wears glasses.'

I felt no shame or sadness
No feeling of involvement,
What once caused shock
Is now the norm.

Dear God with years of blood
and blasted human flesh
of funerals and pleas for no retaliation.
Endless platitudes from priests and politicians
How do we care again?

I hear Donne's words
'Every man's death diminishes me.'
And know that the uncaring of this man's death
Is my diminishment.

Forgive

Jane Wooton

What if.....?

A kiss, a stroke
a whisper in the dark
awkward movement
clumsy fingers fumble
feel so good, sore that time
feel so good.
A moan, a sigh
one, two, three, he's inside
hurts at first
it's alright now.
Starts off slowly
builds up fast
a steady rhythm
free at last, free at last
A kiss, he's done
she wants more
he closes his eyes
begins to snore
Darkness comes, she feels alone
doubts begin
to pinch inside
just suppose ..... no, close your eyes
felt so good, but what if.....
.....would you stay with me?
He doesn't hear
felt so good, but just suppose
My God, but what if.....?

Brendan Harper

That's Entertainment

Mine's a pint and a Large Black Bush,
come sit a while and talk my friend,
Aye alright mate, no need to push.
It's me your pal the bottle here.
Did you see the match, Jesus wasn't it crap,
it's been some time since last we met,
To find the goal, that forward needed a map.
Perhaps avoidance is your game,
Did you know, Vitamin K help clot the blood,
but you are mine.
I'm a very smart guy, as well as a stud,
the quivering hands til you feel my touch,
Cause I can make love for five straight hours,
the bitter yellow bile that stings your throat,
And my body is covered in manly scars.
None can appease but your friend the bottle.
I can win at rugby, after a gallon of beer,
your love of life, and your life of love,
And I know a great joke, about a Nun and a Queer.
Are both governed solely by my whims.
I'm the sort of guy the whole bar adores,
your courage and your fear are one,
And if women dislike me, they're Lesbians or Whores.
Masked only by my cloak.
I'll dig deep in my pocket, to buy all a round,
so come my friend and sip,
But I'll knock mouthy drunkards straight to the ground.
Sip deeply from those cupped hands,
Mine's a pint and a large black bush.
As one again, as should we be.

Samuel Curry

Inquisitive Child

Inquisitive child
Unsullied pages
Unwoven by interconnecting
Threads of time

Inquisitive child
Questing probing
Weblike encounters
Inexperience sublime

Barbara Brown

Silence Beneath the Grass

At night I place within my thoughts a story of silk and gold,
A thought beyond a whisper, a shiver beyond the cold,
In reaching out for wisdom through brains of smudge and mirth,
Tears that fell upon me long before my birth.

Tears that drench my soul from beyond the sacred land,
The wealth of being poor, the warm and bloody hand,
The fear of not being scared, the wound without the pain,
Are left in words of wonder on a storm without the rain.

To feel the ancient thunder is all but one too brave,
And left beside the roadway, the primrose and the slave,
To grip the burning coal in a conscientious fist,
The truth will wait in hiding for the rising of the mist.

And feel that be plenty by minds are kept away,
Not one sod dare the field shed to hear the strangers pray,
Not one heart miss a beat lest the blood be old and slow.

For trees that dare be small must die of rot and age,
And ink of every colour must vanish from the page,
For when I leave for ever this spoilt and greedy earth,
The truth write its story on the ashes in the hearth.

Liam McGill

Out of Step

A blackbird rose from a tangle
Of sweet shrubbery. A careless lifting
On a warmth of air.
In the moist, lazy afternoon,
Dregs of rain dribbled from the pines.

I could see them walking towards me.
I could see them walking arm in arm.
His arm in her arm. I trembled.
His arm in my arm. how warm it had been,
How safe, how glorious,
Oh, how achingly brief.

They walked easily,
Carelessly, careless of me.
How could he forget so effortlessly.
His dreadful loyalty had weathered
Tiny cracks in the walls of our joy,
Like frost-water in white plaster.
He said he wished me no pain,
But our first embrace put me beyond
Such immunity.

I stepped bravely along the tipsy path.
We passed, nodded, said 'Hello!',
As one does

Dixie Wilson

Dylan Thomas at Laugharne

Short fat figure muttering to himself
in the isolation of a boat-house
at Laughharne.
Cherubic face deep in thought
Dark curls falling over a furrowed brow.
Pencil poised
Heavenwards.

Drawing deeply on the Woodbine
squeezed between bulbous lips.
Brushing the ash abstractedly
from his thick Aran sweater.

Gazing out over the estuary, and beyond.
Breathing in the wild Celtic beauty
that is Wales.
Creating line after line of immortal verse
from poetic images and visions
that crowd his mind.
A mind that is
a melting pot
of genius.

Terry James

Mary Kelly

What did the coppers see first, not
the stops on your eyes, they were cut out.
Your thighs stripped, your side ripped
like liver, your liver on the table hacked about.

It was Lord Mayor's Day, another fable born,
A Miller's Tale in a tiny room, no stable.
And something comic in the horror, sex
as death, a live-in lover cursing breath and bother.

Left scraped open, a hand in your womb, half a
split apple and long way from Limerick.

And those girls from Whitechapel, sick and poor,
made love with strangers to keep the wolf from the door.

Gerald Hull

Deserted

He did not come that day.
There was no knock upon the door,
No blue eyes smiling into mine,
Just the long dark hall,
No more.

No further meeting had been fixed, but-
'Tomorrow he will come',
My heart said, and the house
Seemed to lean slightly,
Listening, numb.

The long tomorrows fled away.
The brown sad leaves came floating down,
Cold air wafted beneath the door
From the bleak and lonely town---

In the winter darkness
Crouched by the flickering flame
I think, 'How happy I should be
If he who meant so much to me
Returned again'.

Joan P Moore

Coming up to Oxford

The cancelled ferry booking hit him hard,
hard for a man who took things for signs.
An omen for the shape of things to come?

On deck the Stranraer wind had left him numb.

And shown his rooms, exhausted he'd dismissed
the practiced airs and first impressions now.
So much concerned to keep his native pride,
dignity returned with sleep denied.

Unpacking, something slowly made him smile.
A sense of Cavehill, ironed and neatly piled.
For tea, a 'Big Mac' 'mongst the spires and domes,
as far away from Brideshead as from home.

T P Burgess

Intellectual

People are
starving all
over the world.

'Is that
 a symbolic statement?
Do excuse
the alliteration!'

Headline
in a local paper:
'Well-read man found
dead in public library
- drowned whilst
looking for
submerged meaning
in
seven-word statement.

Alliteration
not ruled out'.

Paul Hutchinson

Deacinee II (1990)

What will become of us who are transplanted,
Our roots dug up, placed in a soil untilled
By us? Time makes familiar the changes:
The words we know, but not their meaning here
Spoken as poetry from the people's lips,
The myths an legends glimpsed through twilit mist
And most of all, light, and the landscape grips
Our hearts. We have been lulled to feel
Our new roots strong, sustaining, well-grown, real.

But twenty years of violence and discord,
Of hundreds dead, each one a nucleus
Of sorrow;
Rigidity of thought, and prejudices
Unaltered through the years;
The Celtic richness claimed by some - rejected
By others; all this brings doubts.
We are again uprooted: our new roots
Poisoned by old contamination of the soil.
We are outsiders still.

Joyce Neill

Retrospection

A fly buzzes angrily on the window pane,
Trapped between folds of lacy, white curtain
And its own outraged reflection.
Are you aroused by the unwelcome thought
Of a secret rendezvous you may not keep?
Or painfully reminded of another, caught
In gossamer web, sticky with death?
Your own out-manouvering of an irate spider?
So greedy now for life, that you dare not
Waste one second, in another entanglement,
As I open my window, and you are lost
In air laden, heady fumes of diesel exhaust,
I hear buzzing of flies from
Drowsy afternoons, soaked in the
Fragrant sunlight of long ago.-
When, in the peaceful hour before tea,
After the cooking and clearing away was forgotten -
Flies settled on the warm window pane,
And joined Grandmama in sleep.

Margaret Steele

After Enniskillen

Day ends
And night silts in across Lough Erne,
Turning the waters to wet ink,
Blotting the sedges and fields
Which patch the gloom on the distant shore.
Dark winter forlorn.
Nothing stalks the rushes now.
Even the heron has gone
And grebes and moorhens sleep,
Chill-feathered in frost.
Black on black the margins dim;
Tangle of willow and alder
Merge with blackthorn
And I know not where I am.
My landscape is lost.
Those sheets of sweet water,
Once lucid and pale,
Now reek of sour cordite,
And bruised over with pain.
The cold flotsam of violence
Congeals in a stain

Jane Wright

People's Marathon

Pheidippides, why did you go so far?
Was there pain - there is now -
But I am nearly finished,
Just round the next turn and
Then I shall see in the distance
The last bend and from there, the stadium.
Just about another five miles.
I haven't been fighting the Persians;
No heavy spear and shield do I carry:
Why should I worry?
But it's painful, can I make it?
That bloody stitch, breathe deeply,
Run through it, can't stop now.
All that training, what a waste, keep going
one, two, three, four'; good it's gone, thank God.
Hope I don't get shin splints or cramp
Like that poor sod lying there:
I knew he was going too fast.
Damn those cars, keep out, give me a chance.
Crowds gathering, oh no, keep the road clear.
They're cheering me; wave, smile - was it a grimace?
'Only another mile, you'll make it.'
That's me they're shouting at.
Yes, I'll make it, if I have to crawl.
Zatopek, Bannister, Pheidippides and I,
We have done it but my message is not just for Athens,
It's for the world, urbe et orbe,
I have done it, Everest, The Channel, The Marathon.

Patrick Waters

Annalong Harbour

An awful smell
the stinking, rotten, corpses
of the has-been fish.
The disgusting sludge
the smelly gunge
awaiting its putrid prey.
It if pounces we are sucked
underneath the sludge!!!
It was disgusting - the old fish heads
and the oily scum on the top layer
Dead amongst the fish heads.

Neil Andrews

Mirrors of Time

Come Grandpa, sit by the fire,
Tell me of days,
with your long-winded ways,
of how thanks used to be,
but are no more.

Come, Grandson, sit by side,
Tell me of days
with your exuberant ways,
of how things are to be,
But not for me.

Father and Son, come sit close to me,
Between the parallel mirrors of time,
the infinite images of future and past,
unfold the story of all mankind.

Pauline Ogilvie

Misconception

Mother, I am shielded, safe and warm
Not yet born.
My heart, eye, ear and thought share yours.
We are one.
I and countless others anticipate our births.
We know not hatred, greed of power
Nor death, nor war.
We, protected, gently float in amniotic balm
With love and peace.
Come Birthlings all of multi-race
The world awaits.

Mother, is all well? Your heart's fast beat,
Is that fear?
I sense a shadow in your eye and thunder
In your ear.
You think of me. I feel your call of love.
You wish my birth.
I'm eager for the world of promise, love and fellow men.
Mother I am here. I'm born.
No womb, what then?
Love? Peace? No. The shadow grows.
The world
Destroyed!

Maggie Smith

Northen Ireland News

The button's pressed to cut off another horror,
More blood on the pavement awaiting it's crown of flowers.
Bewildered sickened I seek the mundane task
Slide into the easy routine groove
Away from the ever present pain
Feeling these conflicts will outlast me.

But in the winter weary garden
The snowdrops provide shine.
Delicate white bells bending before the wind but not snapping.
The hard knots of tension loosen.

Joan Millar

Moonrain

I'll walk on the rise of the road
where your rivers can not touch me.
Where only the rain wets my feet
and only the wind drys my face.
I'll walk through leaves and dung and lichens
to the end of the shore or rise of the hill.
But stars alone are my witness
and only the wind holds my hand.

Jenny R Whatmough

Scraping Bones

Today I refused to be governed:

getting up late
I washed my clothes
drank a pot of
coffee by the fire
then read a little
replaced a bulb
and idly watched people
go by.

you should read
the other poem
that I have just written.
its about scraping
flesh from bones
and how marow
warms the belly
like soup.

Gary Hughes

Untitled

We met and embraced with our cheeks and our arms
and we separated and talked.
Never once did our eyes meet in this discourse
As we talked of what had gone before.
About all those years that we hadn't met
Had we cared at all?

My heart turned over and I thought
How wrong I was to come.
This social farce completes the ending
of two to one.

And then I looked, not glanced
at the face I had once so loved.
And I knew your spirit was escaping,
seeping from all of your senses.

You, your spirit was struggling free,
to meet with mine that was constrained,
by social graces, pain and fear.

The eyes met, the spirits embraced,
tumbled, danced, spoke their words
of lure.

I was being courted again,
of this I am certain and sure.

Marie Therese Lundy

Token Entry

In the time that it takes to fool my sight
I've already seen what I was looking at
Even if response is only cause and effect
I can still tell you what it is I've seen
But even when
The friend of my best friend
Looks straight through me
She smiles as she cuts through me
With no thought or reason or understanding.
And I shout: 'Hey, Mr Wheel,
Spin me a thread, and weave it.
Weave through the lives of these people.
The one's I've touched.'
But deep down he knows
That I'm standing by the corner
Of Innocence and Time.
The streets flow away from me in directions,
But which directions, I cannot comprehend.
A friend of my good friend
Still snares me, can fool me
The sky is that misty blue colour
Y'know the type that clouds your mind
With dreams (or is it demons?), but,
Now the friend of an old friend
Shares a smile with me, as I choose
love instead of innocence
Moments rather than time
As I exchange now for then,
And my mind squeals for sleep.

Chris Allen

Without Form

Grey shadows
against the walls
the ashes of passion

fragments of the night before,
paler, growing smaller in the
deadening whiteness of light and sun,

one touch tells you
you're alive,
my reflection
shows me I have form

for just a second
I thought I belonged to sound,
a lifeless thing with a spirit,
a stone filled with voices

darkened by hollow shade
grey shadows against the walls,
the ashes of passion,
fragments of the night before

paler,
growing smaller
in the deadening whiteness
of light and sun.

Kathryn McCone

Seriously

She gave him the nod,
A couple of drinks, I'm anybodies.
Three, 'she swore' Everybodies.'
He bought the forth,
Nodded towards the door.
'Oh! That's a joke!
I'm not to be taken,
Seriously,
Seriously.

He watched the panic
Dying in her eyes.
Not at all surprised,
He knew the score.
The door was too far away.
Maybe another day would dawn,
But, probably not
at all desirable.
Seriously.

James Watson

Plucked Flower

A hand carelessly plucked a flower
Vicia Sativa
From the nurturing field.
Sending paralysing fear
to a million creeping things.
A hand tenderly plucked a simple tune,
La Paloma
from the voluptuous guitar.
Giving enervating joys
to lovers lying in the grass.
Gone they were within an hour
player and his maid.
Letting silence move
the million creeping things
To forgetfulness of a ravished flower.

John Simms

Castle in the Air

Getting my own back is a castle
In the air. Her love was a lie,
And she admitted that much by believing

The broken teeth of Kinbane
And Dunseverick were a giant's doing.
He strode in, looking for trouble,

Killed the McDonnells and MacQuillans,
And playfully hid the bodies,
Limb by rigid limb, under the landscape.

Now Dunluce soars above me-
I'll not come down to the sea again
Through this nest of ghosts.

I can't cope with the rigmarole,
The weeping, the calumny, the murder,
If that's what it is, of a name.

Howard Wright

Eclipse

I watch you through the stained glass window as you walk across the road.
Your fingers are wrapped deftly around the books you carry.
Your movement is slow - unhurried - the November drizzle speckles your wind blown hair.

Oh to reach out and touch you! - to say -
Wait! - stay awhile.
But on you walk and I am helpless and alone - unable to break down the barrier between us.

A shaft of sunlight darts swiftly through the pane, reflecting on the wall in shades of red and gold.
I am momentarily distracted - I look down to where you once where - you are gone - a figment of my imagination?

Now, like a filament of light having shed its glow, only darkness remains.

Sharon McCleery

At Parting

I could not know how it might feel
If you were gone.
An inner chill like frosted steel?
Nights' waking hours too long
And stripped of sleeping?
Perhaps it would have meant
Some warping of the mind, keeping
An underlying discontent
Through all the fabric of the after days
And life bereft of hope or praise.

Instead, I find food tastes the same,
The moon still rises
Through its cloak of stars and still the rain.
The wind surprises
Dry whispering heaps of leaves;
And, as before,
White-ribboned waves recede
Reform and wallow in along the shore,
My eyes still feed
On morning skies, cloud-shadows on the hill
But all is dead within
Unquiet, storm-racked or dustlike still
For you are gone,
And all is dead
For you took with you all the song
And everything that mattered
Or was precious.

Claude H Bigg

Divided we Fall

In callous continuity -
We fall.
Likened long to dross
From life's autumnal tree.
Soon fusing with
Earth's dust -
Atoms. mingled millions;
Mortal rust -
Like leaves long left alone,
Made to moulder
Upon the killing fields
Of Ulster ground.
In hues of Orange and Green -
We fall.
Irreconcilable in life,
We become, by death, inseparable!
Our tribal - flags,
Our blood-soiled symbols,
Accounted as dung -
Marking nought
To our merit,
Before the Great
White Throne
Of He Who judges souls.
In street and field -
We fall.
The reaper respects
No soul,
Nor social situation;
As he with
Cowl-covered grin,
Hopefully hovers over
Head of hapless victims.
Greedily he waits
For the fool's pull
Of triggered demise.

We fall, Friend, we fall.
We fall, Foe, we fall
Oh, who will help to end
This deadly autumnal season.

Cornelius Kenny McClinton BA

Our Cat

Descendant of Bubastis,
Worshipped in old Egypt,
Goddess of hearth rug
And arm chair.

A whiskered egoist
And aesthete
As bland as butter,
A torturer

Of mice and birds,
Docile on the knee,
Soft furred and sensuous,
Addicted to massage.

A nibbler of ears,
When affectionate.
A claw-raker
When tail-trodden.

Flatterer, liar
And petty thief.
Sycophantic stroker
Of human shins.

A Messalina
Of the dustbins,
Piercing the night
With lustful ululation.

A file-tongued,
Cream-guzzling
Fish-enamoured
Green eyed slut!

Lilian R Morrow

The Trespassers

Like a foot print in moon dust
that neither rain nor wind can
ever erode the mark remains, and
while he dwells in moth-deserted
corners of the darkness is it she
who flits between the causeways
of his dreams, running gnarled
naked fingers through rock-pools
or peering with fanlight eyes
into the tangled webs of thorny
hedgerows, fancying she'll find
there something to forgive?

Ann McKeever

Magilligan Point

Here there are posts stuck in sand.
Knuckled knots, whited like bone,
hard and splitting on the grain.

Here there is barbed-wire stretched,
rusting with salt-blown spray,
keeping nothing from nothing.

Here there are sharp-pointed grasses
curling their edges inwards
keeping fresh water to themselves

and freshly succulents
distilling
their bitter saps.

Here is the hiss of dry sand, swept
by a wind that carries the distant
call of a high soaring gull.

Here is a lonely place where
a prison and a firing range
are the only signs of the human race.

David Fullerton

In Commemoration (of Patrick Kavanagh)

I sat beside you on your seat today,
Bronze Bard of the Common man.
In nearby Grafton Street your verse he busked
from his bill of fare, A La Carte poems for the shoppers there

My son sat on your knee today.
He touched your nose and hat, I didn't think you minded
as you stared into your still, dark redemption.
I wanted to touch you but feared you'd startle and leave

The sculptors hands have shaped
you well but missed upon your greeny shell
one thing...
no clay upon your boots.

Gerard Callaghan

The Ballad of the Forgotten Heroes of Perpetual Emotion

Allan took an ordinary plate in his hand
In a frenzy of sexual frustration
He raised it above his head
In a haze of dense tears
He smashed it over his fraught cranium
Painlessly he took a shattered piece of this plate
Plunging it deep into his tendon
He saw his childhood as clearly as the fresh blood
Bouncing off the Barcelona dust
Realizing that his proud Grandmother's eyes
Lay in that wispy vapour trail
He took pages of his teenage bible
And burnt them, singeing the expectation of his lofty
Forefathers
Realizing that the eyes of youth closed before birth
He coughed in the thick vapour trail
Of forgotten jets and childish reflection
Reaching into his used jacket he found an empty cigarette packet
And smoking the contents, he thanked me for the lift.

David McMechan

The Shy Man

Tentatively he came in
Shyly listened.
I beckoned him toward us.
A shy man,
A gentle man.

Music shaked, agreed upon.
Then as I looked
you both exchanged fiddles,
retained bows.
Musicians etiquette.
The delicacy of the 'handing over' affectionately.

Hopeful abandon.
A little bit of your genius played on unknown strings.
Your fiddle in this strangers hands.
Peacefully he smiles
as his bow glides along your dancing strings.
The shy man.

Clare Toland

Full Cycle

We scooped spawn from the spring dam,
Slippery! Slimy!
Big bulging blobs of embryo frog,
Like sago into a saucepan.

We placed the spawn in a big barrel -
A big grey, galvanised barrel
And waited ..
Waited until full stops became commas
And commas became exclamations that darted in the depths.

Then as sure as the vernal and autumnal,
In the proper order of things,
We witnessed our own equinox -
Fully formed frogs!
Repulsive creatures,
Absurd amphibians!
Grace grown grotesque,
Beauty become bizarre.

I was glad when they leapt to freedom,
Relieved when they vaulted voluntarily out into the swaths of grass.
Next year we would dip into the spring dam for their spawn.

Elizabeth M Wiseman

Obituary Days

Brightened flats where silken people move
Attract the night. Envious and watchful,
We claw at the shadows
On the ridge of thought.
Ambitions range the corners of our eyes
Beyond our reach. We miss them,
Always, always miss them.
In loneliness we miss them.

My Mother hated drink.
And I recall
The silence
And the smell of whiskey
In the house.

My Father drags his bad leg
After him, slower than
An act of treachery,
Arrogant in pain,
Token of division.

Superstition hatches in the bar.
A plastic greenery enhanced
By luminescent light
Sheens in the swimming barsmoke.
We drift in colour, drinks in hand.
Two men caress a card machine
Menage a trois
With promises of warmth.

In our dark eyes
We register the flashing blues and reds.
Back in the corner,
So many women make women sounds
In garish secrecy. they
Rustle touch caress and lounge.

A love sponged out,
Thoroughly, respectfully, like stains from leather.

On this one day
Public grief marked by timeless verse
And fond regrets. Line after columned line,
Breast-pocket memories lie exposed,
Killed by...killed for...suddenly...at home,
The daily roll-call of the daily dead.
In memoriam we perpetuate their shattered lives,
Cheap at eleven 'P' a word, those paper windows.

Seamas Keenan

Atlantic Drive

Sometimes when you
Look at the Sky
Synged pink
by evenings
breath
Or talk a walk
by the Sea
Barefoot through
Seaweed tangled
Waves in Sensual
tease
advancing
Subsiding
The oceans Wet
frothing mouth
Licking your
feet
gasping
The drowning
Light
Watching it Fade
The moon rising
The blueness of night
filling your eyes
your head by
Sea salt
intoxicated
A mystic moment-
Felt once.
Remembered for
Eternity.

Marie O'Brien

Ritual

Turnip purple face
Chest merged with belly like a lambeg drum
He lolls at the ring wet bar
Buttocks drooping from a thin stemmed stool
His pint of Murphy's
A small thing in a rough edged fist.

Nightly he drinks
He stays till the closing call is made
Not quite sober when he leaves for home
Lumbering, cautious in his tread
Not quite drunk he makes his nightly stop
A hunger born of stout must be assuaged.

His mother lets him in
Old, she knows better than to nag
That journey's done
He slumps in the easy chair
Filling the room with beer and vinegar smells
She makes him tea --- silently
He is all that she has.

Jack Leathem

Between Joy and Pain

The archetypal pallor of his face
Illumines leaves as yet uncut;
Pale blue breath imbues
The common objects in his room
With silent symbolism.

An arch of ochre wall
Surrounds and elevates
A shimmering crimson sail;
Significant in its solitude
The restless raft of longing.

Antique heroes, unquiet souls of myth,
Sound their distant bell;
A single note of beauty
Enriches the silence,
Anointing the evening hymn of his brow.

Unworthy the ones
To whom such gifts are given,
Who draw the curtain of the miraculous
Across the lighted window of the natural.
Undeserving, the melancholy traveller
Who, smitten with yearning by that dim glow,
Surrenders to a promise.

Mark Shields

After the Storm

Stumps of trees
gravestones buried in the hillside.

Tree trunks unemotional
lingering undertakers.

Decaying leaves
withered wreaths.

Branches scattered
mourners straggle.

Kathleen Carville

On Inishmacsaint

From the soft squelch of mud
That spatters the ragged shore
Rises a gradient trod by centuries
Of feet that leave no trace.
Raised stone is etched in memory
To the light that shivered and failed
To abandoned beliefs
And forgotten wreaths
On darkened Inishmacsaint.

Sunday service is attended
By a congregation of cattle
Disinterested hooves tread heavily
On the unmarked graves of the lost.
And the only sound in the wind
Is the wheeze of an iron gate
Of haunting Vespers
Of half-heard whispers
On darkened Inishmacsaint.

Gary Law

Lily

Lily your dark secrets grow
Down by the Willow pool,
with wisps of air
under coloured birds
your reflection lets you know,
Lily covered in the shade
bless the golden morning,
young men's hearts are up for sale
in your latest escapade,
Lily sweet as virgin soil
the footprints have been covered,
in your life you see no darkness
and nothing you could spoil,
Lily in the Lilac trees
your magic is so gentle,
the young man lies in paradise
where only you can please,
Lily your dark secrets grow
down by the Willow pool,
this morning they all looked for you
but no-one seemed to know,
Lily by the Willow pool
late in the evening sun,
why do you only sit here
when the air is soft and cool?
Lily by the Willow pool
Lily in full blossom,
you have entered Autumn
and it is soft and cool.

Ronnie Orr

The Book of Dreams

Dreams past, dreams present,
'Vanity, vanity
all is vanity' said the Prophet -
Wise man.
'Dreamer of dreams,
born out of my true time' said the Poet.
Born too late, or too early?
Nothing seems to fit,
we are the dreamers,
the outcasts and the loners,
Alone in a crowd, some mad,
others too sane, united
only by rejection.
The best are poets,
Prophets, philosophers and Artists.
The worst lie in gutters.
When I was a child, I dreamed
of what might be, now my dreams
are filled with what might
have been. Two pages of a book
stuck together and turned
as one, a missing chapter
which contains the key
to the whole plot.

Kevin Byers

Tor

You once asked me what the Ailsa Craig is:
It is omen, dolmen, dark rock force,
Tourist attraction.
Its bullet snub loaves out of the sea,
An oceanic bannock,
It is disturbing because we
Are all surface shifting and noise,
Mood and movement.
Minds counting seconds
Cannot cope with granite:
We have no words to sound
Those subliminal coal-old depths
If 'Tor' is the correct technical term
Thank God for it:
At least it sounds old and blunt
And dumb enough.

Maurice Macartney

Nothing Left but Songs

Feelings,
I can't afford the confusion
distorting my daily life,
destroying the illusion.

Words,
so natural in everyday life
have no meaning in this vacuum,
random thoughts run rife.

Bodies,
once intertwined with passion
become jerky and awkward,
it's the moment to cash in.

Memories,
an eon of beauty and fun,
the last laughs on me
clouds act swiftly to cover sun.

Radios,
reminding me of our wrongs
caught every fleeting moment,
there's nothing left but songs.

John-James T Nisbet

Liberty

Immense conception,
Yet too minute for consciousness.
Consigned to a hidden existence,
Precious burial in a womb.
Considerable or expendable?
When does life begin?

A murmur, a flutter,
Foetal feeling or foetal fatality?
Consent,
Consolation.
Embryonic desolation.

Jacqueline McVeigh

From the Hill

Now here' s a peaceful spot;
You could weave your web of Sunday walks
Round these small roads
And over friendly farmer's fields
And see the City spread her jewels
In the evening mist.
Never noticing the small flashes
In the bare streets off the Shankill
Or feeling the dull thud of the car-bomb
Blasting splinters through the ragged fabric of life
Which hangs like tattered washing
In the battered backstreets of this tail end of Ireland
(Land of saints and scholars and gentle people weaving their web of Sunday walks.)

K Lynn

Sam

I watch you shuffle towards the gate
to perform your nightly routine
with that little broken padlock.
I recall the day when
with conspiratorial glance,
you admitted me to the secret of its brokeness.
It was just camoflage
to fool them in the dark.
I see you on some long past evening
set sail on that grand bicycle
for bright lit up places
and the warm glow of whiskey.
Spending the money you had about you then
from the sale of fat lambs.
Sam this ain't no glorious summer,
I long for the sun and you sitting out,
me surrounded by daisies in the grass.
Maybe we'd talk warmly about the days
of horse carts, the flax, and potatoes in lazy beds.
But I know you will stay indoors
talking away to yourself or perhaps ghosts
of the thirteen who once shared that house.
Instead we will talk of violent acts
supposedly carried out in our names
by lesser men than ourselves;
punctuated by remarks about the weather
and grievances about your relations.
I wish we could talk only of heart things
then perhaps we might capture
something of the preciousness of our being.

Terry Rainey

Not Conscious

Not conscious, he's laid out on the screen
Limp on canvas then to a wired bed
The last round-up, they shut down machines
Bells will ring for in seconds he's dead

It's not to be trivialised
But in doing what he lived for he died
He tested himself to destruction
Having climbed near his peak of ambition

I would never do it myself
But then I would never hang-glide
I've truly examined in depth
The sensations spectating provides

Not conscious of me being cruel
Through admiring endurance of pain
It's consensual challenging duel
And I will watch boxing again.

Colin McGuigan

Daughter

No mirror
But a reflection
A part of me
That is not me
I speak to myself
And hear my angry answer
And see my puzzled eyes
We strain to understand
Ourselves.

For I am she
And she is me
A chance to start afresh
And yet no chance
For she is herself
A new beginning
No worn-out repeat
We look together in the glass
And we are four.

Joanne Griffith

On the Sixth Day Before Christmas

Hailstones batter
The front street
As the wind roars
Over the rooftops;
There is a thin white
Carpet in the garden
Revealed by the
Neon city lights;
And my thoughts
Relate to sleep
As I survey the winter storm.

From the east
There are flashes of light,
And thunder rattles
The hemisphere in moments
Of darkness;
Beyond this all is quiet
For the populace
In the main
Are asleep
As the clock
Strikes three a.m.

What mystery lies
In the elements?
What power!
What threat!
The age-old Gods
Of mans evolution,
Overthrown and superseded
By the Son
Of a Jewish maiden,
At whose commands
The elements obey.

Liam O'Comain

You're Mistaken

Looks no different from you, or me
Has only one head, not two or three
Civil tongue in his quite pleasant too
Wouldn't harm a fly, that's what they said
Ah no not him, the maker of dead
Spoke to me he did indeed, bid me the time of day
You've got him mixed up with somebody else,
Your making a big mistake
Pushed my car the other day when all around forsake
I don' t believe you, I never will
Not Billy, not Micky, they couldn't kill

A J Smyth

After Hours on a Winter's Night

Walking home through the fog
with thud and crackle;
a conversation ends
and people part laughing.
The drone of cars approaching,
quickly passing me by,
patting the road furiously
humming an ever-changing note.
The bark of a dog echoing
down a dark hollow street
and the distant click and scrape
of heels veiled in the night
marching in time to a female pitch.
Shivering, I adjust my collar
and lengthen my stride homeward
toward a hot cup of coffee
and much needed rest
from the over-indulgent city.

Thomas Brennan

End of the Tunnel

Hope and life, ebb and flow
Like the waves of the ocean
Shifting the sands of time

While light at the end of tunnel
Like a misty mirage in the desert
Beckons beguilingly on

We urgently scurry towards
Infinitesimal scraps of nothingness
Infuriatingly evasive
Maddening insubstantial

At one moment blindingly brilliant
Hope crystallised! Ambitions realised!
The next, vicariously vanishing
Into cloudy blurred uncertainty.

And then. . . . . . .
Looking back over one's shoulder
At the illusion of a bright beginning.

Arlene McCullough

The Dilemma

Like a proud flag in a spring breeze,
Unfurled resplendently he marches,
Upright through his glorification.
The trappings of a mundane existence,
Filtered through the careful vocabulary,
Of a certain station in life.
In the short step between the office and the coffee shop,
You can smell the cultivated indifference of necessity.
The large and empty words, the precise posturings,
The skin-stretched mask of his disguise.
Revealing more of the dilemma than it discloses of the man.

Mr R D Bartlett

Midnight

Midnight says the clock, the magic hour
That many poets verse their thoughts upon
And write of moonbeams, dreams, and wishing star
And the romantic coming of the dawn.

Midnight all is well the poet cries
He cannot see really, not he,
His hand can't pen the ugly poem that lies
Beneath the beauty he prefers to see.

Midnight nightmare hour, the hour of fright
In shadows, evil lurks with jaws agape
To swallow up the sinful deeds of night
The murder, lusting, robbery and rape.

Midnight says the clock the final hour
And poets long to write of fantasies
With not a single thought of things that are
And were, and will be cruel realities.

Matt Lamb

The Light at the End of the Tunnel is Fading

I saw a man yesterday.
The trees blew distorted in the wind,
His face was worn and empty.
Leaves fell and died.

A child lay on the pavement.
The rustle as a bird alighted,
Her hands lay fragile, torn and shattered.
And church bells rang.

A man waved a flag and spoke of war.
I stared at the hills,
Three men had just been killed.
Sun glinted off glass.

A woman stood on a wall.
The sea crashed down,
Selling her god.
Children danced and sang.

A father died.
Fire burned quietly in a dark room,
No-one noticed.
Coals glowed silently.

Niall Liaran Balmer

From the Lock Springs This

Away in a land unknown to me, staring wide at a beautiful
familiarity, the house is surrounded both front and back by
visions of home, yet this is peaceful.
Strangers faces smile as we pass, and I see friends behind
a visage never seen. A glimpse of the past, a living of
the present, and an insight for the future. It's all the
same. Does anything change here?

The only change is from snow to Spring, from ripeness to
bareness.
Then there is youth progressing through time and the
ageless wrinkle and change. But there is a beautiful
slowness in life, time to see and think. The crowd doesn't
push your thoughts here, instead they spring from
nothingness and potter inside you with an unknown freedom.

Paula Sharvin

Mistaken Identity

I mind reading once, and thought it was queer,
for nothing that's like it could quite happen here,
of a German who worked for a firm making prams,
in the thirties it was, the place is unclear,
but the factory was huge.
each section supplied a different part,
yet all so worthwhile,
and all the more so when his wife had a child
and needed his help, he duly obliged,
and slipped round the plant while taking great care
he couldn't be seen, and moved here and there
to take a part home,
and when he was ready, on night when alone
he started to build.
Each piece was so precious he just couldn't wait,
though the going was hard and the evening was late
he still carried on his labour of love,
that spoke to him hope, and then of a dove
that cooed to him patience,
and joy it came through as he put it together,
the innocence too, that preceded the shock.
It didn't relate to the work that he did,
each part they supplied,
on their own so demure, and yet were sublime
when one would consider the end was in mind.
But this was so different, the look of surprise,
He couldn't believe the sight of his eyes
When he was done, and looked down the barrel.
He assembled a gun!

Clive Maxwell

A Homecoming

The safe walls of my childhood surround me again,
All that I've seen and heard in these last years
Has brought me to this end.
I pray for one empty page that I might write and read these things again
And I write by the light of a clear blue moon.
Over my shoulder, in through my window it fills this room
And if ever I felt I owned a thing, this room is mine,
But more - the memories that dance on the blue-white walls
As I clap in delight from my bed.

The grey hair that twists among the brown seems not my own
For I am too young - ageless in myself - to be marked so,
They prove only the marking of time,
But I, thank God, am not so tired.
Deep within me memories of myself throb as one, as a single strum
Humming with life - yes, even the eldest is here with me now,
Stirred and stirring again,
I stop my pen that I may watch and see
And know and feel I'm home again.

William Vincent

Christmas Again

A December day remembering ways
we laughed.
We could not see beyond the lights and tree
we loved.
Like figures in a crib we followed stars.
With innocent eyes we looked on our Messiah
Now just as his, our boyish looks are gone.
In Bethlehem they murder on the streets.
Thoughts of flocks and shepherds
we merely borrowed.
Reality signs above some door we missed

But present wrapped, delights
and glittering cards
Windows lit and tinselled trees of pine;
Welcome sights for wishful eyes remind me
of a time when it was Christmas
and I a child.

Kevin Meehan

Mother

You bore me,
heavy-bellied
with warm endurance

You drew me
tiny beetroot screamer
into light and touch
and sound and smell

First gaspings
you saw me,
nurse thumped me, inhaling
growing me, up tall and strong
added pain, and somehow laughter
and all I ever did
was hurt and not consider
you infinite, sunrise-caring
Now though, is Mothers Day
and see the possibility
of me without you.

James Hay

Dreams Stole

Trees sweet trees
Hair that sways with the breeze and
Eyes so sad
Mirroring the image of
Mind to soul
Dreams stole.

Bitter the winds
Cosmopolitan grins have
Lost me within
Lips so sensual
Seducing my mind into
Loving you prone
Existing alone
Dreams stole.

Susan McCarron

Offsprings

Each time you turn your head,
I see in you
Myself.

Eyes that challenge every word.
My mirror image
Looking back.

You argue well and I can't win
Because the words you use
Are mine.

I find in you the faults in me
Two stubborn minds can blindly love
But rarely agree.

Una Walsh

Shopaholic

Among the smart footwear
A floor mirror beckons.
Her shoes look so awful-
'I need a new pair.'

In the hairdresser's window
A mirror reflects her.
Horrors of horrors-
'I need a re-style'.'

The fashion department-
Mirror walls everywhere.
How shabby she looks!
'I need a new outfit.'

Home to reality-
Face retribution-
'It was mirrors that made me!'
'You need a psychiatrist'

June McGuire

Just a Glimpse

Just a glimpse, in a passing crowd,
Of face you seemed to know.
But it's only a trick that the light has played
On a memory of long ago.

Yet your mind goes back, and you live again
That time, when one you knew
Was a very precious part of your life,
And the sky was always blue.

But time moves on, and years go by,
And that special friend has gone
And even though time heals the pain,
The memory lingers on.

Life can be sad, and yet be glad
Two pathways crossed for a while,
And in your heart throughout the years
You'll keep the ghost of a smile.

Amelia Wilson

Hometown

Grey, one-street, doubled-camped and boring,
Divided along lines
Of hastily erected steel and wire.
Provincial, local, colloquial and closed in.
Small minded people
With alleyways of acceptance.

The stone-cold monuments,
Grey, red,white and blue,
Where D.M. boots and U.V.F. tattoos
Idly strut proud,
Holding bottles of wine
Wrapped in brown paper bags.

The brick wall by Dunnes,
Red, green, white and gold
Where army coats and Celtic tops
Languidly stand firm,
Holding bottles of wine
Wrapped in brown paper bags.

Depressing and stiffling,
It longs to close ranks,
A prospective student that
Went to the bad,
And the broken glass
Of ambiticus dreams
Lying shattered on the corner
Of Woodhouse Street.

Gareth Hughes

Memories

Trapped inside a memory
Of best forgotten dreams,
that tear apart ones sanity
and rip away the seams,
of
hurt that is not healed enough
to make a fresh start.
To
hide away the loneliness that
makes the days so dark
So
that is why it is best to start
a diary of the heart.

Bernadette O'Reilly

The Death of Charlie, my Friend

Charlie I loved you, old rogue that you were, I studied your suffering. You knew, and I knew, you were living out the last months of your life. But Bridget must not know. Little Bridget, girl of your heart.

Now shaking with the 'Parkinson'. Your eyes said, 'How am I to leave you Bridget.

You need me, your tears and your fears keep me ever bound to this earth.

Until I hold your hand once again. Free from the shackles of these worn out bodies. Free to wander and be in that place of beauty and peace.

I have seen in my dream-deaths'.

Charlie I miss your physical presence.
I thank you for the time after your death, when you stood beside me and touched me with joy, a 'thankyou for the care and attention I gave you in your life.

The first Sunday after your death, it pained me to see no fire in the hearth of many fires. No tea in the pot. Just little Bridget, cold and crying, bewildered at the loss of her lover and companion of fifty years.
The fire in the hearth burns bright again Charlie.
The Kettle is on the boil.
We reminisce, Bridget and I, she going over your last hours in disbelief.
I laughing at your carpet slippers and quick loss of temper.

You are not with us Charlie
And yet again you are
For Love and Memory are stronger than death.

Rose Gallacher

Helicopters

Whirly-gigs my father called them:
'There's one of them whirly-gigs'
He would shout, shading octogenarian eyes
As a puma, wessex or gazelle
(The lynx had not reached Ulster then)
Clacked above the cottage
On its way to Bessbrook or Crossmaglen
Bristling with fresh troops
For the changing of the guard
On some besieged hillside in Armagh.
There noisy frequency kept him company,
Kept from thinking long
or lapsing into a second childhood.
;I mind the time,' The signal
For some confused chundering
Of a tale half a century old
Would mercifully be edited out
By the throb and suck of rotor blades.
Helicopters were a God-send,
Restoring reality, re-establishing the mind.
He learned their names and shapes,
Bought books on the subject,
Became an expert.
The night before he died
The first lynx flew over.
He never heard it,
Never saw the pointed snout
Or the metallic sleekness
Swooping, night-black
In the failing light.

Roy Gamble

Then and Now

Years later, faded photographs reveal a
laughing, longing, handsome, carefree youth reading
A paper, squinting at a sun which too soon
Disappeared, leaving a chill which hardened the
Spontaneity of youth, stiffening your
Features to manhood and masking you with reserve.

Why could I not have known you as you then were?
You, whom often since I have regarded the
Loneliest man who ever lived. Shrouded by
Reserve, you seemed to spurn and shun love, though on
Reflection, every dutiful action spoke.
We, your children, as we grew, avoided you.
Long silences prevailed. We could not wait to
Leave and soon we did. You left unwillingly,
On your lips our names, which meant to you just what?
Why could I not have known you as you then were?
And what, now, would you have thought of me today?

J C Nelson

Sky

Broadening horizons,
Gazing stealthily at open spaces,
Far beyond the view of man,
With a need to see deep,
Into the moody places,
Of mind and soul in combination.
Co-ordinated to a point,
With a fully blossomed meaning
Embodied within time,
Taken from the soul,
Resounding and moving for one,
With a fulfillment evermore held.

David Warwick

October Footfall

October morning
Silently rejecting moons remnant
Discovers the heart of me-
Disowning summer
She weaves her charm
Tracing a map of fragile images
On the canvas of my soul
With an indelible tangle of sounds
Smell and memory
Stencilled in gold-
Starlings wings
Wood smoke
Filigreed leaves delicately ochred
Spiders webs
Caressed with Octobers dew
Cling to me
Contentedly,
Knowingly
Nudging November.

Anne Steele

The Lad from the Crewe

He wooed her he won her he said 'love is true'
He promised to wed her the lad from the Crewe
Like a fool she believed him then what did he do
He upped and he left her alone on the grave

Her eyes they were wet and her throat it was dry
Her head felt like bursting she thought she would die
When like a swallow he bid her adieu
She prayed he'd return once again to the Crewe

And so now my daughter my secret I tell
To protect you from heartache perhaps shame as well
When a lad comes a courtin' take care what you do
Just in case he's a son of the lad from the Crewe.

Elizabeth Quinn

Windy day

Turned leaves
Rolled petals
Torn webs
Field prisoners
Pulled waves
Puffed shirt
Ruffled bird
Shadows and light
Washing, wishing
Wooing wind
Mating tree with tree
Flower with flower
Yet in jealously
Against its nearest rival
Bee tumbles the bee

Rosemary G Carter

The Ghost Horse

There's a ghost horse in the woods
Among the dripping Spanish moss
Spreading in white, eerie movements
In the spirit of the cold biting frost

He's there in the leaves beside you
Silent and prancing in the fog
With lustrous black eyes protruding
He leaps over rotted dead logs.

His whinny is loud and piercing
Breaking the silent night air
Glowing bright and luminous
Taunting 'Catch me if you dare.'

He rears catching rays of moon light
Standing longlimbed arrogant and proud
Then suddenly all is dark and quiet,
And he is gone with a passing cloud.

Kerry A Watson

Stolen Sun

I stole your sun:
though I wanted you to be free,
I used to hate to see you smile
unless you were smiling at me;
I'll smile no more in a short while,
Miss Honeybun.

I don't deserve
to be alive in the same world,
to walk the same ground every day
as such a life-preserving girl;
to get to hear the things you say
of those you serve.

Now we must part
before we even get to kiss;
you'll ne'er know what you meant to me,
and how I longed to show you this.
The only girl this century
to steal my heart....

Apart from one
I'd rather forget ever smiled,
who made my life so meaningless;
those foolish days we never whiled,
those hours we never shared in bliss,
she stole my sun.

Kevin Connolly

Our Native Land

In the wake of it all
Is it worth the tears that roll
The hearts that are broke
The children who choke
The bombing brigades
The hoods with guns
Everyones involved
Mother Father Daughter Son.

In my perfect world
There's no barricades
No tanks and jeeps
No guns to shoot
No graves to fill
No politicians to lie
But my perfect world
Is only in my mind
The dead may get there
But we're left behind.

R Humphrey

A Wasp in November

Its time for you to die now,
Summers gone, a summer that
Will remain in my memories.
Memories of the quiet morn-
ing madness. Another phase
gone. The last leaf on the
tree. Yes old friend die
graciously on my clothes
scattered floor. Your my indic-
ation that summers gone,
for well perhaps another
year.

Thomas G Baxter

Poet's Weapon

The poet's soul is not private
It gets the urge to share
Each time it pains or glories
Blank pages won't bare

The heartaches and the triumphs
The loves that now lie dead
Childhood fears live on and on
That should be put to bed

The poet has to labour
Expose scars of the heart
Until each hurt has been expelled
The new day cannot start

Emotions leak from pen to page
In rhymes of harmony
And soon it all lies waiting there
For any eyes to see

They say the pen is mighty
Mightier than the sword
I suppose when you come to think of it
It's easier to take the top off a biro
Than draw Excalibur from the stone!

Jacqueline McGregor

Love?

The fear is vicious
Never ending
Revenge - the taste
Is bitter sweet.
A kick in the teeth
Is a bitter pill
Love in itself
Is the greatest hope,
The worst fear,
The dearest truth,
The nearest shoulder,
The deepest soul
Speaking to soul,
The best emotion
But the hardest to shake off.
After the fall
The pouring out -
Fall apart
Or fall out.

Sarah Anne Hill

Adoption

You gave birth to me,
You gave me life,
You gave me a name,
You gave me up.

I wondered about you,
I wondered where you were,
I wondered why I was adopted,
I wondered how.

You disowned me,
You didn't want to know,
You never came to find me,
You can now.

I finally traced you,
I made you aware of me,
I hoped you'd want to meet me,
I know it's in vain.

You still disown me,
I can't understand why,
You are frightened who'll know,
I am proud of you.

I can keep your secrets,
You can keep mine,
I just want to know you,
You need to know me.

You must feel something,
I know I still do,
You are my natural mother,
I need you.

Suzanna Lynn

A Love Unknown

I have loved no-one but you
And still you defeat me.

Paul Robert McAvoy

Untitled

Examine the hand that reaches in support
There may be no arm behind it!

Deirdre Eastwood

The Watchman

I stand and gaze upon a scene
of strung barbed wire, of iron gates,
Hedgerows, trees, and lawns of green.
And just beyond the iron gates
People walk and talk, and lovers stroll
hand and hand.

And past me, roll lorries, full
of giant rubber tyres that encircle
wheels of steel
And when they pass, the summer dust
clouds that rise.
Hide the green lawns and trees from
my eyes.

Iook and watch for what seems to be
an eternity
And wait for my belief to come.
And when he does, he too, will stand
And look and watch and wait
And he too will silently hope, like me
that nothing will explode or burst
into flame.

William James Coulter

Our Queen

She looks down on everyone, who passes by.
She sees many sights, and hears many things
she has felt the snow, and rain, and wind.
Heard laughter and seen many tears
she holds her head high and stays
silent thro' it all.
Our Queen Victoria watching from
our City Hall

Jonathan Crawford

Christmas Again

and no turkey on the plate
Pardon our poverty
but we've no plate either.

Just a loaf would do, a loaf of bread
to take away this gnawing dread.

Keep us the bones and crumbs
you kind-hearted people of the north.

Send your dogs away hungry
that we might live, and let
the cats chase vermin again.

Tell our rulers to be fair
and give us all our proper share.

And under the blazing sun
where our children are dying
and men and women are dying
can't you hear the vultures confide
in each other
and call off their quarrelling
now there's more than enough to go round.

Ivan James Casson

What if I Fell in Love with Her

Inspired by tales of impotent men
And wasted chances given air
A scornful lash that hides despair
Allows the face to smile again
The taunts and gibes of long ago
Return to play their weary song
A trusted friend who doesn't know
The tried is trite and the going gone
Forever. And ever and ever they'd say
We said we'd be friends to our living day
Our coils kept apart while our soul embraced
The words of my eyes were all that kissed
Your multifoliate concaves; a kaleidoscope
In chequered crimson, and journey
Between shadow and hope.
Eyes unadorned playing tricks with the soul
With lips turning down
Sketching ends that reveal
That the lines fade to grey
And the caves are a con for the vex that I feel
For the fruit I can touch
But forbidden to peel

Mark Crooks

Gracia By the Sea

In Gracia's gaze I'll stand a while,
just to watch as time slips by,
like the ships passing the harbour and the fishing smell.
By the whitewashed cottage,
sits Gracia looking old and well.
In time I imagine, with the fishermen and sea,
I will old like Gracia be.
To wish like her, again to be
Young and silly, like the child who speaks his mind.
In the audience of the hot summer sun,
and the screaming seagulls,
wheeling in the warm inviting sky,
in Gracia's gaze I'll stay for just a little while.

Paul Charman

Untitled

Your being watched
We have a very choosey cat,
She wears a pink bow,
She takes the best pickings,
Like mummys diamond ring,
Puss puts it in a swag sack,
Along with a running trophy,
And a large bottle of gin,
Yes our puss is choosey.

Lara Crozier

Through the Barrier

Thud! thud! huh! huh!
Breathe out,
Arms pump
Feet plod
Heart throbs
Sweat pours
Muscles ache
Effort ...

Thud! thud! huh! huh!
Eyes dream,
Mouth smiles
Head nods
Knees bend
Body moves
Heart lifts
Exhilaration ...

Eileen Monaghan

Only the lonely

My love lay dying
As I whispered in his ear.
Salt tear to cheek, crying
As he strained to hear
Last soft words of loving.
'I love you, be brave'.
My heart is lying,
now within his grave.

Anne Withenie

Why Have I Kept it?

Why have I kept it?
A barrow, bottom-rusted after forty years,
Deflated tyre, up-ended in a bramble patch.
Sometimes recalled, like pastured steed,
To tumbril to their compost deathbed, grass and weeds.

My early vigour powered its black and shiny frame,
Which groaned as heavy-burdened wheel sank deep in ground
About to be transformed, from dank rough-grazing fields
On West Belfast's Black Mountain flanks, into well-loved
Surburban garden. Its sides reverberated
With the thump of soil and broken flags. The children
Rode in it. *Why have I kept it?*
It holds golden *youth!*

Transported to second home in furniture van,
Riding at pensioned rate, all active service past.
Prideful place reserved, since leaving it behind was
Quite unthinkable. Its presence - a conditioned
Reflex of countless stresses shared successfully;
Talisman - to ward off future 'green' disaster;
And comforting reminder of former garden
Lore - enough to plant anew a *second* Eden -
(Though - like that ancient ship's crew of elderly Greeks -
Whose captain lamented the passing of the years,
We'd long since lost our 'strength which in old days moved *earth*
and heaven'!) *Why have I kept it?*
It holds silver age!
And now - its upturned idling wheel
Is a circle of memories!

S A McElroy

Chameleon

Snow as a white blanket on a bed of the most beautiful;
The conversing of the robin and its song radiant;
The crunch of the snow underfoot.
Snowmen.

Punctually nature's complexion is changed;
The apprehension ionises the air and
Hibernation sets in.
Darkness.

The only hint of colour left is that of the various
Hemispherical ciboriums bobbing up and down
Along the crowded grey briefcase avenues.
Ignorance.

Soon the mutation seems perpetual as
Infected elastic fluids steam from
Diseased hearses.
Poison.

The Chameleon's wound is now obviously septic,
Its illness adding to the peoples' perplexion.
Has time overcome the decrepit
Grey Chameleon?

Cormac R Kernan

Islands

Dogs and sunsets would never be the same
Nor sun, nor moon, nor noise of freezing water
Tall trees scratched on moonlit skies
The sound of birds flying homeward ... calling
For you and I had moved to new dimensions
Were love transferred without the spoken word
Let each the other touch immortal soul
And reached a place where you and I were one

Yet now
Encircled by our shattered dreams
Surrounded by the broken promises
We are as like
As lost
As
Jesus.

Stanley James Goudie

Emerald Now Ruby

The blood of innocence ran freely.
For the moment, no more,
Murdered from birth by history
Replayed each day by all.

The just are just men no longer,
For the word is but a mask,
Hiding torn hearts and laughter
And the results of the Devil's scorn.

The land of Emerald turned ruby
For the shroud has a new place to stay
In the skies above once green fields
Turned red by the scent of our dead.

Tony Corey

The Gift

And it's not love that you have to
Bind me tight to you
- it's a passion for sure.
An obsessive desire
to own; and I, unsure
Become
When I belong to you
it seems you want it to be;
Out of reach
of those tendrils, catch me;
I am helpless
Insignificant, I fall.

I don't mind, now that I know
but will I always know.
Perhaps some day I'll find myself
Aware of some lost.
I'll be yours and forget
who used to be.
Slightly shell-shocked,
no longer think of me.

Pauline Matthew

Circumstances

Is it early, or is it late
In our wee place, time has no date
Nowhere to come in and nowhere to go out
Just going around and around and about.
Caought in a chamber of darkness below.
Just flowing to and fro, in this endless dome
No glimmer of light to show us the way out
Whispers bounce oft glass sides within
Is she right or is he wrong, from side to side it goes on
Not a spark or flicker of light
So around and around the hatred goes
Until the glass dome explodes.
Then we realise we're in a glass dome of a bigger size
So around and around we go again
Is there no end.

Brendan Shields

Work Out

Soft lines part company down, dragging her form around.
Bones crunch, out of time and out of mind,
shattered she strikes her life.

Just for sport shooting pool.
The green beige, with pockets leather six abound.
Eight year new to every day, runs into each night,
then passes the old factory light,
where forces came no work now stands.
Derelict smashed windows, a factory stands.
Water logged a mist crept in.

Shadows lean tall, but some times not there at all.
Coming down the factory walls, seeping as it fell.
Pale moon rises there to above barbed wire fences,
gates locked to a working sound.

Inside looking out, a city on the brink,
down dark alleys sharks fish with knives and stick.
Caught there on Fifth Avenue, an ambulance came to
take the body away.

Every one just looked on, then most drifted away.
the youth with a lisp crying, for buckets of tears,
mostly they thought he was insincere,
the tears just kept flowing.
The shoes she wore leaked with the cold American snow.

Ten minutes later streets under the heart shaped
windows shattered to the calls of a dying cat.
The sun rays melt snow were a death knell.

Michael Boyle

Lost Innocence

Where do the children play
On damp November days,
When mists and rain eradicate
All natural forms and shapes
And leave a blur - ?

Think of the endless summertime,
The freedom and the joys sublime.
When everything is sharp and clear
For those who know no pain or fear.
And no thoughts of doubt occur?

Helen Torr

The Culling

The sight of death still lingers,
fermenting in my head, clouding my
dreams of what might be.
For beneath the misted street lamp
cones, the seeds of hostility still
fester.
For there upon the paved plethora,
stained with stencilled limbs, a body
sprawls cloaked in florid blood.
It lies amid a ring of sickened faces,
swarmed by men in black, draping dragging
sweeping him away from piercing eyes and
clicking tongues.
But it never leaves me.
The image and the sounds of madness are
echoed in each pathetic sentiment issued
in Ireland's name.

Sean C Toman

Untitled

Are you too, looking at this moon -
Great orange orb hung just above the corn,
The golden corn that stands in stacks
Silent and forlorn?

Do you see, as I see,
In your mind's eye
Such a moon as this
Hung in such a sky

Long, long ago and us two, close
Gazing on that sight
Of orange moon and corn-sheaves
And fading light?

And do you stand as I stand,
Silent and forlorn
Thinking of that other moon
Above that other corn?

Helen Quigley

Untitled

The stars that light the darkness
Sing songs of sweet romance,
Their eyes observe the dancers
In love's eternal dance.

Come dance with me sweet darling
Beneath the starry sky,
Let the beauty of your body
Beside my body lie.

We've longed to know each other
All longings in time grow ripe,
Come dance with me my darling
To the song of the stars tonight.

Gilbert L White

War is Announced

When I looked out the window he was still running,
leaving me with only one to love.
Down to the path to the road where the gate lies,
flying away from me and his unborn child like a dove.

Come to me, come to us, return once again,
to embrace us with your injured arms.
There you go off to show your bravery in battle,
I cry for you and pray to God you'll come home to the farms.

Tinya Rennie

Dawn

Grey light;
Grey dark;
Colours faded from around,
Waiting the paintbrush of Day.

Grey trees;
Grey sky;
Birds suspended in silence,
Day will restore their voice.

Grey grass;
Grey air;
Nature lies muted,
Night past, Day is yet to come.

Bright light;
Birds sing;
Colour touches the world;
Dawn has brought the Day.

Joyce Williams

17 Ferguson Drive
(the exact shades of meaning)

Meanings, elusive slipping through our minds like
soap,
Grasping and seeing meaning dart away,
inaccessibly.

Fathoming feelings speaking truths half known.
Grasping the solid ground of opinion
And have it crumble away beneath my hands.

Walking a tightrope of discovery,
Without a safety net of fact.
Stumbling like a drunk unsure of his perceptions
The St. Vitus Dance of defence.

(the difference between tripping and stumbling)

Voices, bubbling softly
Trying out illusions, delusions;
Gently coaxing ideas from the oyster of self.

Revealing pearls, created while
Disposing of the irritating grit of thought,
From grey flabby flesh of ego.

Maurice Milligan